GROSS BUGS™

Cockroaches

Jonathan Kravetz

The Rosen Publishing Group's
PowerKids Press™
New York

To my parents, for encouraging me

Published in 2006 by The Rosen Publishing Group, Inc.
29 East 21st Street, New York, NY 10010

First Edition

Editor: Jennifer Way
Book Design: Ginny Chu

Photo Credits: Cover, pp. 1, 5, 9, 10 Clemson University - USDA Cooperative Extension Slide Series, www.insectimages.org; p. 6 © Karen Tweedy-Holmes/Corbis; pp. 13, 18 University of Nebraska, Department of Entomology; pp. 14, 14 (inset), 21 Daniel R. Suiter, The University of Georgia, www.insectimages.org; p. 17 © Anthony Bannister; Gallo Images/Corbis.

Library of Congress Cataloging-in-Publication Data

Kravetz, Jonathan.
   Cockroaches / Jonathan Kravetz.— 1st ed.
      p. cm. — (Gross bugs)
   Includes index.
   ISBN 1-4042-3043-2
   1. Cockroaches—Juvenile literature. I. Title.

   QL505.5.K73 2006
   595.7'28—dc22

                                            2004025420

Manufactured in the United States of America

CONTENTS

Slimy and Fast

The next time you flip on the light in the kitchen, look out! You just might see a cockroach. Cockroaches like to hide in warm, dark places, such as behind kitchen stoves. They have hard, slimy **exoskeletons** and long **antennae**. They can move quickly, and some kinds give off a bad smell.

Cockroaches belong to an **order** of **insects** called Blattaria. There are around 3,500 known **species** of cockroaches, and scientists are still discovering about 40 new ones every year.

Some cockroaches are household pests. They live off food, trash, and water in people's homes. They **mate** quickly and are hard to get rid of once they **infest** a building. The most common kinds in the United States include the American, German, and Oriental cockroaches.

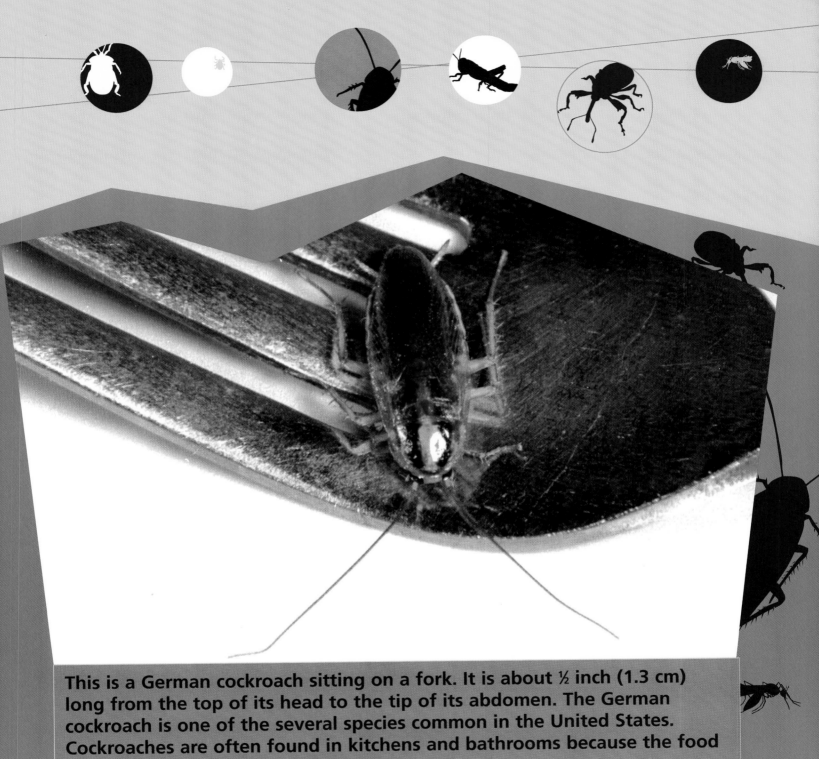

This is a German cockroach sitting on a fork. It is about ½ inch (1.3 cm) long from the top of its head to the tip of its abdomen. The German cockroach is one of the several species common in the United States. Cockroaches are often found in kitchens and bathrooms because the food and water in these areas draws them.

In the wild cockroaches look for places with peeling tree bark or warm, wet leaves on the forest floor. Cockroaches can be found just about everywhere in the world. This cockroach lives in a forest in Trinidad, an island in the West Indies.

Catching a Ride

Cockroaches have existed for about 340 million years. Some scientists think cockroaches may have made up 40 percent of the insects in the world during that time. Today's species of cockroaches look a lot like the first cockroaches.

Today cockroaches make up less than one percent of all insects. Cockroaches are found nearly everywhere in the world. All cockroaches search for tight spaces in which to hide. Domestic, or household, species prefer cabinets, cracks in walls, and gaps in floors.

Cockroaches have spread across the world by hitchhiking. Sailors have unknowingly carried cockroaches on their ships. In modern times cockroaches have been known to hitch rides in airplanes and in travelers' suitcases.

As do all insects, cockroaches have a head, **thorax**, and **abdomen**. A waxy exoskeleton covers their body, and they have two pairs of wings. Cockroaches breathe through tiny holes along the abdomen called spiracles. These bugs have eyes that allow them to see in many directions at once.

Cockroaches have six hairy, spiny legs that increase their sense of touch. Each of its feet has claws that are used for climbing and special pads to help the cockroach move over smooth surfaces.

Cerci, which are two sensors on the back end of the cockroach, act like movement detectors. The cerci can sense the smallest movements of something approaching. This feeling warns the cockroach to run away.

The hairy spines on the cockroach's legs (*inset*) aid in their sense of touch. This helps keep cockroaches aware of approaching enemies. Then they can act quickly and get away. Much of a cockroach's insides are what is called a fat body. This stores energy. If you have stepped on a cockroach before, you may have seen this goopy, white stuff squirt out.

9

Cockroaches will eat just about any type of food that has been left out. Here this cockroach is eating a cracker. Cockroaches are also eaten by many animals. In Africa the female jewel wasp lays her eggs in the cockroach. When the eggs hatch, the young jewel wasps eat the cockroach from the inside!

10

What Cockroaches Eat and What Eats Them

Cockroaches will eat just about anything. Besides eating food people leave behind, they will eat bark, leaves, paper, skin, leather, dead insects, and, in some cases, other cockroaches. German cockroaches can live for one month on only water.

Many animals eat cockroaches, including fish, frogs, lizards, birds, scorpions, and monkeys. Many insects also hunt cockroaches, including army ants and centipedes.

Cockroaches have special ways of keeping themselves safe from enemies. Some species use **camouflage**. Others have sharp spines on their legs that they use to protect themselves from enemies. Some can also spray a bad-smelling mist. Cockroaches are also quick. Most kinds can run about 3 miles per hour (5 km/h).

Cockroach Eggs

Cockroaches go through three stages in their lives. These stages are egg, **nymph**, and adult. The process of changing into these stages is called **metamorphosis**.

The egg is the first stage of life. The female passes the eggs from her body into an egg case, called the ootheca. The Cockroach eggs grow inside the egg case. In some species the female carries around the ootheca. In other species, such as the American cockroach, the female leaves the ootheca in a safe place.

Females can produce many offspring in a lifetime. That is one reason cockroaches spread so quickly and are so hard to wipe out. One egg case can hold about 40 eggs. This means that a female that lives 5 months could mate about 8 times and produce around 320 young.

This female cockroach has the ootheca, or egg case, attached to her abdomen. It can be seen on the far left in this picture. In many species the female carries the ootheca like this.

13

Nymphs are nearly white when they first hatch, like this American cockroach nymph. After each molt the cockroach's exoskeleton grows, hardens, and darkens. As they go through their molts, nymphs' wings begin to grow. *Inset*: This is a front view of a newly molted American cockroach nymph.

Nymphs and Molting

Cockroaches hatch between 15 and 90 days after the eggs are laid. Young cockroaches are called nymphs.

Nymphs grow by molting, or shedding their exoskeleton. German cockroach nymphs molt 5 to 7 times, going from 5 to 14 days between molts. It usually takes them 50 to 60 days to reach adulthood.

When it is time to molt, the nymph gulps down air. This causes its exoskeleton to break apart. The nymph then sheds its skin. After molting a nymph is pale, weak, and wingless. It changes quickly, though. The nymph gulps more air, causing its new, wrinkly exoskeleton to stretch. The new exoskeleton soon hardens and darkens.

GROSS FACT

Once a nymph completes a molt, it eats its old exoskeleton for the protein. Protein is important for growth.

Mating

Once a cockroach reaches adulthood, it can mate. Many cockroach species have mating habits. In some species the female takes a position known as the calling stance. From this position she produces a strong chemical called a **pheromone**. The pheromone, carried on the wind, can draw males from as far away as 30 feet (9 m). Males detect the pheromone using their antennae. Males can also let out a pheromone to draw females.

When the male finds a female that is ready to mate, they face each other. Then they touch each other with their antennae. Then the male **fertilizes** the eggs. Cockroaches can mate many times in their lifetime. Some cockroach species have longer lives than others. Some species live more than a year. Others live only a few months.

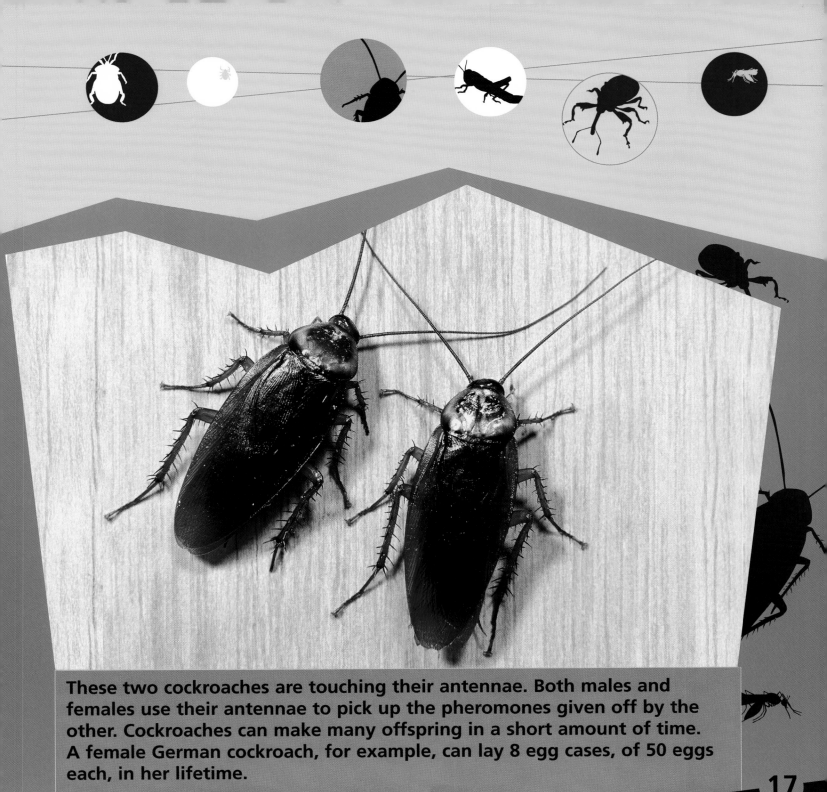

These two cockroaches are touching their antennae. Both males and females use their antennae to pick up the pheromones given off by the other. Cockroaches can make many offspring in a short amount of time. A female German cockroach, for example, can lay 8 egg cases, of 50 eggs each, in her lifetime.

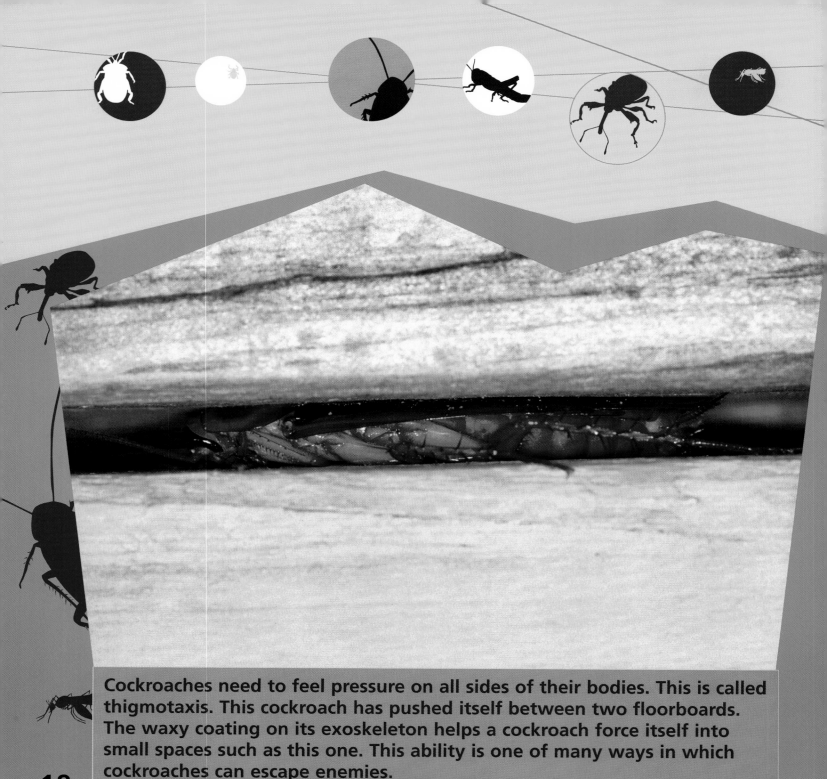

Cockroaches need to feel pressure on all sides of their bodies. This is called thigmotaxis. This cockroach has pushed itself between two floorboards. The waxy coating on its exoskeleton helps a cockroach force itself into small spaces such as this one. This ability is one of many ways in which cockroaches can escape enemies.

Thigmotaxis

Adult cockroaches like to feel pressure on all sides of their body. The term for this need to be in tight spaces is thigmotaxis. The narrower the space, the more they like it. The cockroach's waxy coating **evolved** to help them slip into gaps and cracks better. By slipping into small spaces, the cockroach can avoid enemies.

Cockroaches are not easy to kill. The cockroach's brain is spread throughout its body. Because of this cockroaches can live up to a week without a head. They will finally die of thirst.

GROSS FACT

How much do cockroaches like close spaces?

In 1983 in New Orleans, a woman suffering from an earache went to the doctor. He found a cockroach living inside her ear. When the doctor looked in the other ear, he found a cockroach living there, too.

Cockroaches and People

Many cockroaches carry illnesses that they can pass to people or other animals. In addition cockroaches leave behind **excrement**, molted skin, and partly eaten food, which can cause **allergies**. Between 10 and 15 million Americans suffer from cockroach-related allergies. Only dust causes more allergies.

Domestic cockroaches can infest homes and are very hard to get rid of. If nothing is done to stop an infestation, a cockroach population can grow so large that some cockroaches have to move out in search of new food and spaces. That is how an infestation can spread.

This sticky cockroach trap has caught a few dozen German cockroaches. They were trapped in a single night in one house. An infestation can include many cockroaches, and cockroaches are hard to kill. It often takes several attempts and many methods to get rid of an infestation.

How People Fight Cockroaches

People have many ways of fighting cockroaches. The easiest way to avoid infestations is to keep living spaces clean. That means storing food in airtight containers and keeping trash in lidded cans. If cockroaches cannot find sources of food or water, they will not stay.

Another way to kill cockroaches is to set traps. Inside the traps are sticky surfaces, so the cockroach cannot escape. It is also possible to poison cockroaches. The poisons in these products come in low doses, so the cockroach will not detect it. After eating the poison, the cockroach dies over a few days. This does not always work because over time they can become **immune** to poisons. This is one of the reasons cockroaches have been around for millions of years!

GLOSSARY

abdomen (AB-duh-min) The large, rear part of an insect's body.

allergies (A-lur-jeez) Bad reactions to certain things, such as animals or pollen.

antennae (an-TEH-nee) Thin, rodlike organs used to feel things, located on the head.

camouflage (KA-muh-flaj) A pattern that matches its surroundings.

cerci (SER-sy) Two sensors on the back end of a cockroach.

evolved (ee-VOLVD) To have changed over many years.

excrement (EK-skreh-ment) Waste that has passed out of the body.

exoskeletons (ek-soh-SKEH-leh-tinz) Hard coverings on the outsides of animals' bodies that hold and guard the soft insides.

fertilizes (FUR-tih-lyz-ez) Puts male cells inside an egg to make babies.

immune (ih-MYOON) Safe from something, often a sickness.

infest (in-FEST) To fill a place, usually with unpleasant things.

insects (IN-sekts) Small creatures that often have six legs and wings.

mate (MAYT) To join together to make babies.

metamorphosis (meh-tuh-MOR-fuh-sis) A complete change in form.

nymph (NIMF) A young insect that has not yet grown into an adult.

order (OR-dur) The scientific name for a very large group of plants or animals that are alike in some ways. It is a broader grouping than a family.

pheromone (FER-uh-mohn) A kind of chemical produced by an animal that allows it to send a message to another of the same kind of animal.

species (SPEE-sheez) A single kind of living thing. All people are one species.

thorax (THOR-aks) The middle part of the body of an insect.

INDEX

A
American cockroach, 4, 12
antennae, 4

B
Blattaria, 4

C
cerci, 8

E
egg case, 12
egg(s), 12, 15

exoskeleton(s), 4, 15

I
infestation(s), 20, 22

L
legs, 8, 11

M
mate, 4, 12, 16
metamorphosis, 12
molting, 15

N
nymph(s), 12, 15

P
pheromone, 16

S
spiracles, 8

T
thigmotaxis, 19

Web Sites
Due to the changing nature of Internet links, PowerKids Press has developed an online list of Web sites related to the subject of this book. This site is updated regularly. Please use this link to access the list:
www.powerkidslinks.com/bgugs/croaches/